Published by
Medieval Media, Norwich, Norfolk, England.
www.dochurst.co.uk

LEFT: *Panoramic view of the nave Lierne vaulting.*

Norwich Cathedral Nave Bosses

An Illustrated Guide to the Medieval Splendour of the Nave Roof Bosses in Norwich Cathedral.

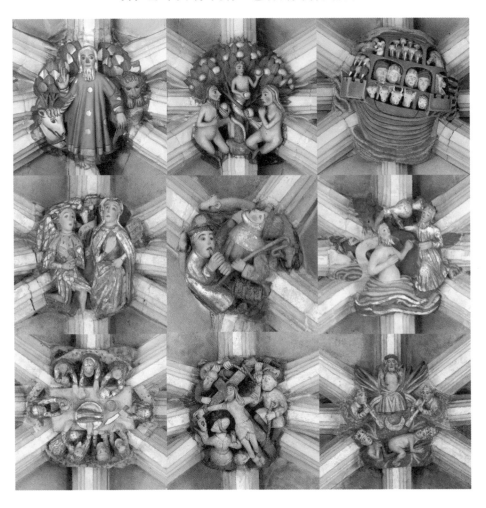

Paul Hurst ARPS

additional text by Phillip McFadyen

ABOVE: *Noah's ark.*

This book is dedicated to my wife, Anne and daughter, Clare.

Published by
Medieval Media, Norwich, Norfolk, England.

ISBN 978-0-9926388-0-1

Printed by Barnwell Print Ltd., Aylsham, Norfolk NR11 6SU

£9.99

Contents

Foreword   6

Introduction   7

A brief history of the bosses   8

The layout of the vaulting   9

NA Old Testament - The Creation   10-13

NB Old Testament - Noah   14-17

NC Old Testament - Abraham   18-21

ND Old Testament - Jacob   22-25

NE Old testament - Joseph   26-29

NF Old Testament - Moses   30-33

NG New Testament - David   34-37

NH New Testament - The Nativity   38-41

NI New Testament - Signs and wonders   42-45

NJ New Testament - The Last Supper   46-49

NK New Testament - The arrest and trial of Jesus   50-53

NL New Testament - The Crucifixion   54-57

NM New Testament - The Resurrection   58-61

NN New Testament - The Last Judgement   62-65

NN2 Bishop Walter Lyhart   66

Bibliography   67

Foreword by the Bishop of Norwich
The Rt Revd Graham James

Norwich Cathedral has many glories, so many that despite our best efforts the exceptional roof bosses in the Nave do not get the attention they deserve from many of our visitors. It is understandable since you do need exceptional eyesight to enjoy (or be slightly scared) by this panorama of the story of our redemption from the Creation to the Last Judgement.

The intricate work done by the mediaeval stonemasons on the roof bosses is a reminder that only the highest quality of craftsmanship was thought good enough for this great House of God. Paul Hurst's stunning photographs and Phillip McFadyen's text means that what we normally see at a distance is now brought near in all its colourful glory. The gospel story is timeless. What was represented in the creation of these roof bosses more than five hundred and fifty years ago remains true to this day. 'Jesus Christ is the same, yesterday, today and forever'. (Hebrews 13.8). What does change over time is technology and the privilege of living in our present age is that a book like this is possible and places the beauty, humour, starkness and wonder of these roof bosses in our hands. We marvel at what we have received. We celebrate these gifts from those who worked and worshipped in Norwich Cathedral centuries ago. We are inspired by their imagination, sophistication and faith.

+ Graham Norvic:
September 2013

6

Introduction

Within Norwich Cathedral there are many treasures. This book focuses on just one, the collection of 255 medieval bosses sitting high above the Cathedral's nave and choir. They look down on clergy, congregation and visitors to tell the story of both the Old and New Testament.

These bosses have been hewn from a heavy stone, with exceptional skill, the details were added by medieval stonemasons using hand tools and techniques that have changed very little over the centuries.

The characters within this stone medium are said to be a snap shot of medieval life with scenes from the travelling mystery plays of that time being the inspiration for the stonemasons. Some of these designs take very little imagination to visualise scenes performed in the streets by actors of that period.

ABOVE: *The medieval stonemason at work with his tools.*

The aim of this book is to bring the stories down to earth from their heavenly setting, and place them in a handy book. The bosses are captured in natural light, presenting their colours and using the light and shadow to give the images more depth and a three dimensional quality.

The descriptions of the bosses in the book have been taken from Dean Edward Goulburn's "*Ancient sculptures in the roof of Norwich Cathedral*" of 1876 with minor alterations. To complement the images Phillip McFadyen has offered a wonderful text giving his unique vision of each bay and the story that unfolds.

It is my hope that this book will appeal to the ordinary visitor and to schools. Both need more access to these images and this publication is offered for that purpose. For those interested in more in-depth information I would recommend the reader towards "Stories in Stone" by Martial Rose and Julie Hedgecoe.

Paul Hurst ARPS
13th October 2013

A brief history of the Bosses

The present stone Lierne nave roof was built to replace a timber roof which was destroyed by fire in 1463, when the spire collapsed into the timber nave roof.

Bishop Walter Lyhart (1446-72) was responsible for providing the new roof to ensure that it would not meet the same fiery fate as its predecessor; for this he chose a stone vaulting in the pattern of a Lierne-star design. In choosing such an expensive material Bishop Lyhart had to sell some of his private estate to cover the cost, as neither monastery nor bishop had sufficient capital. The design of the roof was the work of stonemason Reginald Ely who, prior to this, had completed work on King's College Chapel in Cambridge.

Medieval stonemasons were in high demand at the time. Bishop Lyhart's stone mason Robert Everard was the master stonemason for the Cathedral (1451-85). Everard was given the task of completing the present roof from the designs of Reginald Ely with its collection of 255 story-telling bosses covering both the Old and New Testament, from the Creation to the Last Judgement. The bosses were to remain visible until the reformation when the vaulting was covered in a wash to hide the stories. In 1870 Dean Goulburn had the wash removed which exposed the original colours, since repainted in the 1930's.

The series of bosses appear quite distant when viewed from ground level. The central boss is between 30-40 cms in diameter, surrounding bosses range from 20-30 cms. The depth is the key to their three dimensional quality which the designer took great effort to detail and the stonemason to achieve.

ABOVE: *A view at vaulting level looking west into the nave.*

Layout of the Vaulting

The vaulting runs from the tower passing above the choir and along the whole length of the nave ending at the west wall above the great west window.

N refers to the siting in the nave. The 14 bays are classified alphabetically, so that the last bay is identified as NN. It begins with seven bays dedicated to the Old Testament, followed by seven bays detailing the New Testament. Each bay has eighteen story bosses and is numbered accordingly, the signature or key boss to the subject is central to each set and is numbered 10, the remainder surround this boss and contribute to the story. Below is the numerical layout used for each bay viewed as from below (Nativity bay NH illustrated below).

WEST

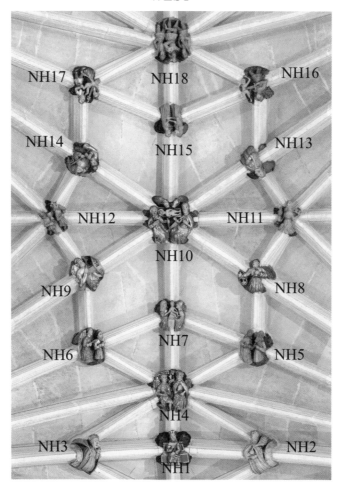

NORTH

SOUTH

EAST

Bay NA Old Testament
The Creation

This series of bosses begins with the Creation as understood by fifteenth century stone masons. They saw this biblical story in pictorial terms and based their images on what they had witnessed in the Norwich Mystery plays. This dramatic tableau was played out on the streets of Norwich by actors. One would have narrated the scene wearing a sun mask another would have dressed as an angel in feathered trousers and wings. God as the architect of the universe presides over his handiwork raising his hand in blessing and ordering chaos with a pair of dividers held in his left hand.

Naked Adam and Eve are handed apples by the serpent who resides in a pot grown tree, another clue to where these images came from. The bosses are nothing but 'stone snap shots' of the plays which would have trundled around the city on carts as the actors dramatised these biblical events.

ABOVE AND RIGHT: *NA10 The fall of man. Adam and Eve tempted by the serpent.*

NA1 The creation of light.

NA2 Foliate.

NA3 Foliate.

*NA4 The benediction of the newly
created universe by God.*

*NA5 Plumed and robed Angel adoring
the Creator.*

*NA6 Plumed and robed Angel adoring
the Creator.*

11

NA7 A white hart, possibly a rebus of Bishop Walter Lyhart.

NA8 Floriate.

NA9 Floriate.

NA10 The fall of man.

NA11 The creation of Eve.

NA12 The creation of Adam.

NA13 Floriate.

NA14 Floriate.

NA15 A white swan spotted with gold, swimming on the water.

NA16 An eagle with red and gold plumage.

NA17 Five fishes of different type on the water.

NA18 The death of Cain.

13

Noah

The image of the ark is the central boss in this grouping based on the Flood story. Genesis tells us that the ark 'rose high above the earth' when the rains fell and so it does in the nave roof, the animals and people looking down on us with some concern.

The satellite bosses around the ark describe the preparations for this epic journey. Noah was able to make a new covenant with God based on mutual respect and understanding, not just between God and human kind but between human kind and the world in which we live. Once back on dry land Noah celebrates by planting the first vineyard. Unfortunately he gets rather drunk on the produce and his two sons turn away in embarrassed confusion.

ABOVE AND RIGHT:
The ark floating on the water. Noah, his family and the creatures look out from the ark.

NB1 Cain going out from the presence of the Lord holding a jaw bone.

NB2 A pomegranate in blossom with its fruit cut open.

NB3 A tudor rose, red and gold , with green stem and leaves.

NB4 Noah building the ark.

NB5 Floriation representing three large pods growing on one stem.

NB6 Floriation representing a pomegranate.

NB7 *Ham exposing Noah.*

NB8 *A man carrying a ewe under his right arm and a ram over his shoulder.*

NB9 *The raven sent forth from the ark preys upon a dead horse.*

NB10 *The ark floating on the waters.*

NB11 *A group of three figures entering the ark.*

NB12 *Noah and his wife leaving the ark.*

NB13 A woman carrying a basket of cocks and hens onto the ark.

NB14 The dove with the olive branch in her mouth.

NB15 A woman parting from a youth.

NB16 A griffin having the head, wings, and claws of an eagle.

NB17 Floriate representing a pomegranate with shells bursting.

NB18 Noah planting the vineyard.

Bay NC Old Testament
Abraham

This bay begins with a stonemason working with his tools which have probably not changed to this day. The red castle or gateway illustrates the tower of Babel and is possibly based on one of the many gateways that were the entrances to the medieval city of Norwich. Here weapons are plentiful in a bay in which the main subject is Abraham. Swords are displayed as we see him preparing to sacrifice his son, Isaac. Some of the medieval delight in hunting and feasting can be witnessed here.

We see Esau hunting a hart and Jacob his brother killing a kid on a stone table. Angels feast with a prepared table before them and Isaac their father gives both Jacob and Esau a blessing from his bedside.

ABOVE AND RIGHT:
The sacrifice of Isaac by Abraham. Isaac is seated on a covered altar whilst Abraham holds high a sword.

18

NC1 Hewing stone for the tower of Babel.

NC2 Pomegranate.

NC3 Pomegranate.

NC4 The tower of Babel.

NC5 Rebecca disguising Jacob.

NC6 Esau returns from the chase.

19

NC7 Abraham entertains an Angel.

NC8 The preparation of sacrifice of Isaac by Abraham.

NC9 Rebecca at the well.

NC10 The sacrifice of Isaac by Abraham.

NC11 One of the Angels entertained by Abraham sitting at a table of food.

NC12 The third of the Angels entertained by Abraham sitting at a table.

NC13 Abraham's servant waiting during the sacrifice of Isaac.

NC14 Abraham's servant going to fetch a wife for Isaac with a camel.

NC15 Isaac at Jacob's bedside holding his hand.

NC16 Esau hunting a hart.

NC17 Jacob killing a kid.

NC18 The blessing of Esau by Isaac.

Bay ND Old Testament
Jacob

The Jacob cycle is given great prominence in the nave bosses. Fifteenth century Norwich owed its wealth to the wool trade so sheep farming was of great interest. Here we see Jacob tending his sheep, counting and separating them and even feeding them. We see him marrying his wives and disputing with his brother Esau. Later in the narrative he is seen wrestling with an angel and being reconciled with his brother. In fact this is an 'everyday story of country folk' with which the citizens of Norwich could readily identify.

Two of the most striking bosses are that of Jacob dreaming and the angels of God ascending and descending from heaven on a ladder. Like Jacob the masons saw this cathedral church as 'none other than the 'Gate of Heaven' and 'the House of God'.

ABOVE AND RIGHT:
Jacob peeling his rods amongst his rams and sheep.

ND1 The cave of Machpelah with Sarah near the tent door.

ND2 The Angel of the Lord pointing out the ram.

ND3 The ram caught in the thicket.

ND4 Jacob journeying to Padan-aram.

ND5 Jacob anointing the stone at Bethel.

ND6 Jacob asleep at Bethel.

ND7 Jacob wrestling with the Angel.

ND8 Jacob rolling the stone from the well.

ND9 The reconciliation of Jacob and Esau.

ND10 Jacob peeling the rods amongst his rams and sheep.

ND11 Jacob betrothed to Rachel.

ND12 Jacob betrothed to Leah.

ND13 Jacob's flock feeding.

ND14 Jacob's goats feeding.

*ND15 Two Angels ascend Jacob's
ladder.*

ND16 Jacob's flight from Padan-aram.

*ND17 The flight of Jacob's wives from
Padan-aram.*

*ND18 Laban and Jacob making a
covenant.*

Bay NE Old Testament
Joseph

The well known story of Joseph is told in this bay with a rich display of medieval hats and costume. We see Joseph's brothers conspiring, finally stripping him and depositing him in a pit, whilst Jacob, his worried father, grips his hands in anguish. One of the brothers conspires with the deceit by collecting blood from a kid, another dips the coat of many colours in the blood in order to deceive his father as to the fate of his son, Joseph.

The final part of the story tells of Joseph being sold to the Ishmaelite traders. Also to be seen is a crowned Pharaoh shown with his sceptre with Joseph kneeling in front of him. This panel extends into the following bay where Joseph's starving brothers are seen running to Egypt and begging for food. The prosperous Joseph stands proudly before many sacks of corn ready to dispense largesse.

ABOVE AND RIGHT:
Joseph cast into a pit by his brothers

NE1 Jacob sending Joseph to visit his brethren.

NE2 Five of Jacob's sons.

NE3 Another five of Jacob's sons

NE4 Joseph going to visit his brothers.

NE5 Two of Joseph's brothers observing his approach.

NE6 Joseph in the stocks.

27

NE7 *Joseph stripped of the coat of many colours.*

NE8 *An Ishmaelite carrying spices into Egypt.*

NE9 *Joseph's steward with one of the sacks of corn.*

NE10 *Joseph cast into the pit.*

NE11 *Jacob's grief on seeing the coat.*

NE12 *Two men and a woman sitting at a table of food.*

NE13 Dipping Joseph's coat in the blood of a kid.

NE14 One of Joseph's brethren killing a kid.

NE15 Joseph is sold to the Ishmaelites.

NE16 Judah interceding for Benjamin.

NE17 Joseph's brethren sitting at a table with food.

NE18 Pharaoh investing Joseph with sovereignty.

Bay NF Old Testament
Moses

The story of Joseph ends in this bay with him standing surrounded by sacks of corn. The narrative moves on with the story of Moses. Here he is seen being placed in the basket by his anxious mother. She launches him into the flowing Nile yet sees that he is adequately hidden in some rushes. Next we see Moses as a shepherd in Midian looking after Jethro's sheep. It is here that he encounters the burning bush and is seen taking his boots off whilst being told by God that he is on holy ground. The burning bush where God appeared to Moses is surrounded by joyous Israelites. An Israelite women looks on as Pharaoh, dressed in royal medieval armour, is seen drowning in the very 'Red' Sea. The doomed Egyptian host, horses and chariots are tossed about in the waves. The mason's attempt at

an Egyptian chariot is based on a contemporary medieval farm cart. Just above Moses with his staff dividing the sea is the Ark of the Covenant carried by two priests.
The Samson saga begins with Samson wrestling with a lion while his parents look on in amazement.

ABOVE AND RIGHT:
The overthrow of Pharaoh in the Red Sea.

NF1 Joseph selling corn.

NF2 Two of Joseph's brothers going to buy corn.

NF3 Two other brothers of Joseph going to buy corn.

NF4 Moses is placed by his mother in the ark of bulrushes.

NF5 Moses taking off his shoes.

NF6 Moses feeding Jethro's flock.

NF7 *Moses and the Angel of the burning bush.*

NF8 *Miriam and a woman with timbrels.*

NF9 *Two Israelites blowing trumpets in celebration of the Exodus.*

NF10 *The overthrow of Pharaoh and his host in the Red Sea.*

NF11 *Two women of Israel looking on at the catastrophe.*

NF12 *Two men with the spoils of the Egyptians.*

NF13 *Moses dividing the waters of the Red Sea.*

NF14 *Pharaoh's servants disapprove the long stay of the Israelites.*

NF15 *The priests bearing the Ark of the Covenant.*

NF16 *Two figures in an attitude of supplication.*

NF17 *Manoah and his wife adoring the Angels.*

NF18 *Samson wrestles the lion.*

David

Once again we start a bay with an overlapping theme. Samson is shown asleep whilst Delilah cuts off his hair. On another boss the flamboyant and quixotic Samson is carrying off the gates of the Philistine city of Gaza. The next subject of this bay is the story of David. Here we see David armed only with a sling tackling the giant, Goliath whose fellow soldiers stand by guarding his extensive weaponry. After David's heroic victory he is shown displaying Goliath's head.

The central boss depicts David's enthronement with surrounding heralds holding sword and mace. Finally, David is seen passing his authority to Solomon while Bathsheba pleads for Solomon their son to inherit the kingdom. Finally, the succession is secured and Solomon is shown enthroned, holding a replica of the cathedral.

ABOVE AND
RIGHT:
The coronation of David.
A crown is placed on
David's head as he sits on
his throne.

NG1 Samson carrying the gates of Gaza.

NG2 Samson bound by Delilah.

NG3 Delilah shaving off the locks of Samson's hair.

NG4 David encounters Goliath.

NG5 Goliath hastens to encounter David.

NG6 Two armour-bearers for Goliath.

NG7 David cutting off the head of Goliath.

NG8 Samuel the prophet or perhaps Nathan the prophet.

NG9 Abimelech enquiring of God for David.

NG10 The coronation of David.

NG11 A herald at David's coronation.

NG12 Goliath's sword being carried at the coronation.

NG13 Nathan the prophet.

NG14 Zadok the Priest.

*NG15 David charging Solomon his son
before he dies.*

*NG16 Bathsheba making request for
Solomon's succession to the throne.*

*NG17 Zadok the priest and Nathan
the prophet anointing Solomon.*

NG18 Solomon is seated on his throne.

Bay NH New Testament
The Nativity

A link is made with the Davidic kingship by beginning this bay with an Old Testament king, priest and prophet. The New Testament story begins with Mary. Gabriel announces the good news while another angel visits Joseph standing with his red staff. The Christ child is shown being presented in the temple whilst Joseph brings a gift of doves in a basket. The angel points towards the Nativity scene with Mary and Joseph.

The Christ child is in a manger with ox and ass looking on. The three Magi and shepherds are seen in the surrounding bosses. Mary is then shown visiting her cousin Elizabeth, elsewhere Herod's men savagely slaughter the children. The callous King Herod is seen dancing with his soldiers.

ABOVE AND RIGHT:
NH10 The nativity. Mary and Joseph are joined at the crib by ox and ass.

NH1 Solomon enthroned.

NH2 Nathan the prophet.

NH3 Zadok the priest.

NH4 The Annunciation.

NH5 Joseph taking to him Mary his wife.

NH6 The Angel of the Lord appearing to Joseph in a dream.

NH7 The Presentation of Christ in the Temple.

NH8 Joseph bringing Mary offerings at the Purification.

NH9 The Angel of the Nativity.

NH10 The Nativity.

NH11 The remaining Magi bringing his offering.

NH12 Two Magi with their offerings.

40

NH13 Mary on her way to the house of Elizabeth.

NH14 Two shepherds at the Nativity.

NH15 The Visitation.

NH16 The Massacre of the Innocents.

NH17 The Massacre of the Innocents.

NH18 Herod's decree for the Massacre of the Innocents.

Signs and wonders

Here we have a group of scenes associated with signs and wonders.
Jesus in the gospels disclosed his nature through a series of events which were interpreted as epiphanies or signs. He is thought to reveal his identity as the Son of God in the following events.

The medieval craftsmen present him in a series of tableaux. Like the children of Israel before Jesus, Matthew tells us that God's Son is found to have sojourned in Egypt. Luke's Gospel has the boy Jesus disputing with the doctors of the Law in the Temple. At his baptism the Holy Spirit in the form of a dove is seen to descend on Jesus. In John's gospel Jesus reveals his nature by changing water into wine at a wedding in Cana. Also in this context we see Jesus raising Lazarus from the tomb and Mary Magdalene demonstrating the Messianic status of Jesus by anointing his feet at a supper party.

ABOVE AND RIGHT:
NI10 The Baptism of our Lord. John pours water from a jug to baptise Christ.

NI1 *The flight into Egypt.*

NI2 *An Angel attending the flight into Egypt.*

NI3 *Joseph on his pilgrimage into Egypt.*

NI4 *Christ amongst the doctors.*

NI5 *Joseph in quest of the Holy Child, resting on his staff.*

NI6 *The Virgin in quest of the Holy Child.*

NI7 The marriage in Cana Galilee.

NI8 A servant filling water pots.

NI9 A servant bearing to the governor's of the feast.

NI10 The Baptism of our Lord.

NI11 A robed Angel holding a robe for our Lord after his baptism.

NI12 Another robed Angel holding a towel or wrapper.

NI13 The first temptation of Christ.

NI14 Our Lord defeating the tempter with the sword of the spirit.

NI15 The raising of Lazarus.

NI16 Two men attending the resurrection of lazarus.

NI17 Two women attending the resurrection of Lazarus.

NI18 The supper in Bethany and the anointing of our Lord.

The Last Supper

This bay is crowded with activity. Disciples carry out Christ's orders to find a room covertly where he and his disciples can celebrate the Passover. We see Jesus and his friends sharing this 'Last Supper' meal and him washing their feet. Meanwhile Judas has gone out into the night to hand Jesus over to the High Priests for thirty pieces of silver. The drama and hurried activity is well displayed in this series of fast moving bosses. John's gospel describes the last Supper in terms of Jesus washing the disciples' feet. There are several bosses dedicated to this and to the feeding of the Five Thousand story told in John 6 which anticipates the Last Supper.

In the feeding miracle all have a foretaste of the heavenly banquet to come. Nothing must be lost or wasted so we see bearded disciples busying themselves collecting fragments of food into baskets and barrels. There is also a young boy offering to Jesus his packed lunch of three loaves and two small fishes. The Last Supper itself is shown as a group of disciples gathered around a fish supper rather than the traditional lamb of the Passover meal. John, the beloved disciple reclines on the breast of Jesus.

ABOVE AND
RIGHT:
NJ10 The Last Supper.

46

*NJ1 *The Triumphal Entry.*

NJ2 *The multitude that followed after the Triumphal Entry.*

NJ3 *The multitude that followed after the Triumphal Entry.*

NJ4 *Access hole used for hanging censing Angel or releasing doves.*

NJ5 *The apostles going forth on their mission two by two.*

NJ6 *Two other apostles sent forth two by two.*

*NJ1 *The Triumphal Entry. The head has been photographically replaced to illustrate the missing one from the boss.*

NJ7 Our Lord sending Peter and John to prepare the Passover.

NJ8 One of the disciples meeting the man with a pitcher of water.

NJ9 Our Lord entrusting the keys to Peter.

NJ10 The Last Supper.

NJ11 A disciple collecting the leftovers from the feeding of the five thousand.

NJ12 Another disciple collecting the remnants of the feeding miracle.

NJ13 Our Lord announcing himself as the bread of life.

NJ14 A young boy offers Jesus three loaves and two small fishes.

NJ15 Two of the apostles preparing for the foot-washing.

NJ16 A figure holding a scroll.

NJ17 Another figure holding a scroll.

NJ18 Our Lord washing Peter's feet.

The arrest and trial of Jesus

Events continue to move on a pace and here we see a number of key characters crowding round Jesus as he is arrested in the Garden of Gethsemane. Firstly we note the lone figure of Jesus praying that he might be delivered from this hour of torment. He asks God to take this cup of suffering from him yet he is content to do whatever his Father requires.

Judas brings the soldiers to take Jesus and there is a skirmish in which the slave of the High Priest, Malchus, loses an ear. We see some of the twelve disciples fleeing as Jesus is bound and taken away to be interrogated by Pilate. There is a good deal of savagery in this bay with the usual fixation on weapons of torture associated with crucifixion. Here we see soldiers with clubs, whips, rods and even battle-axes.

We are reminded that these bosses were carved in a violent age. The vulnerable figure of Jesus is no stranger to such cruelty.

ABOVE AND RIGHT:
NK10 Our Lord before Pilate.

NK1 The agony in the garden.

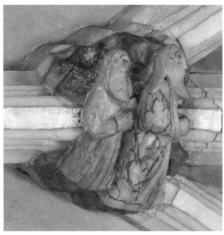

NK2 Two disciples praying.

NK3 Two disciples praying.

NK4 The crowning with thorns.

NK5 Judas leading the multitude to apprehend Christ.

NK6 A servant with lantern and club coming to apprehend Christ.

NK7 Christ led before Pilate.

NK8 Two executioners proceeding to the scourging with whips.

NK9 Two of the apprehending company with swords.

NK10 Our Lord before Pilate.

NK11 Two soldiers engaged in the apprehension of Christ.

NK12 Jews displaying with exultation the warrant for the crucifixion of Christ.

NK13 Two executioners with rods proceeding to the scourging.

NK14 Two soldiers carrying battle-axes.

NK15 The blindfolding.

NK16 Pilate's wife sending a message to him.

NK17 Malchus' ear is cut off.

NK18 The betrayal.

The Crucifixion

The Bay starts with Jesus being led away to be crucified after being arrested, another boss shows soldiers holding the hammer and nails in preparation for the crucifixion. Two men look on, one holding his beard. Jesus is seen here being tied with rope and nailed to the cross; armed soldiers surround this boss. Elsewhere two soldiers are presented throwing dice (casting lots) for the robe of Jesus. Two others are seen soaking a sponge in vinegar.

The central boss shows the crucifixion with many characters surrounding the scene. The next group of bosses shows Christ being laid in the tomb by Joseph of Arimathea and his friend Nicodemus. Two adjacent bosses show two Marys and Mary Magdalene visiting the tomb to anoint the body of Jesus. Elsewhere John, the 'beloved disciple' comforts the mother of Jesus and takes her to his own home.

ABOVE AND RIGHT: *NL10 The Crucifixion.*

54

NL1 *Christ led away to the High Priest's house after his apprehension.*

NL2 *Two Elders.*

NL3 *Two executioners with hammer and nails.*

NL4 *The nailing to the cross.*

NL5 *A soldier tasting the vinegar.*

NL6 *Two soldiers engaged in the Crucifixion.*

NL7 Two soldiers casting lots for our Lord's vesture.

NL8 Soldiers mixing vinegar with gall.

NL9 Two soldiers.

NL10 The Crucifixion.

NL11 Two soldiers.

NL12 Our Lord appearing to Mary Magdalene after his Resurrection.

NL13 *Two of the Marys coming to see the sepulchre.*

NL14 *Mary Magdalene coming to anoint the Lord's body.*

NL15 *The Entombment.*

NL16 *Nicodemus.*

NL17 *John taking Mary to his own home.*

NL18 *The release of the spirits in prison.*

The Resurrection

The story begins with a boss of a soldier guarding the tomb. Others appear in nearby bosses in full dress armour. Next a victorious risen Christ steps out of the tomb surrounded by the sleeping guards. He then stands before a kneeling Mary Magdalene still clutching her anointing oils. Doubting Thomas falls to his knees as Jesus continues to hold his resurrection banner. The rest of the bosses in this bay continue the joyous theme as Mary, the disciples and angels fall to their knees to witness the Ascension of Jesus who is seen vanishing in a cloud of glory with just his wounded feet on view. Finally, Mary is flanked by apostles as they all receive the gift of the Holy Spirit, the Comforter, in the form of a heavenly dove.

ABOVE AND RIGHT:
NM10 The Ascension.

NM1 *A soldier on guard at our Lord's sepulchre.*

NM2 *Two more soldiers on guard at the sepulchre.*

NM3 *Two more soldiers on guard at the sepulchre.*

NM4 *The Resurrection.*

NM5 *St Thomas convinced of the Resurrection.*

NM6 *Our Lord appearing to Mary Magdalene.*

NM7 *Three apostles contemplating the Ascension.*

NM8 *Two more apostles contemplating the Ascension.*

NM9 *Two more apostles contemplating the Ascension.*

NM10 *The Ascension.*

NM11 *One of the Angels of the Ascension.*

NM12 *Another of the Angels of the Ascension.*

NM13 Two apostles at the Ascension.

NM14 Two more of the apostles at the Ascension.

NM15 The Virgin Mary engaged in devotion.

NM16 Two apostles waiting for the descent of the Comforter.

NM17 Two more apostles waiting the descent of the Comforter.

NM18 The descent of the Comforter at Pentecost.

Bay NN New Testament
The Last Judgement

We start with various scenes relishing in the events of the Last Judgement. Here we have the Apostles casting out devils and the Mouth of Hell which swallows the damned. Poor souls are seen being led off by devils, one in a wheel barrow. Others are rising from the dead and being led to heaven. Christ sits in judgement as two angels blow the trumpets proclaiming the day of judgement in which both Pope and King are shown naked.

St Peter is evident with keys sorting out who is for heaven and who is to be consigned to hell. Finally the most holy and glorious Trinity, to whom this cathedral church is dedicated, is seen seated high and lifted up on a throne.

ABOVE AND
RIGHT:
*NN10 The Last
Judgement.*

NN1 Exorcism.

NN2 The power of Christ's people over evil spirits.

NN3 The power of Christ's people over evil spirits.

NN4 The devil thrusting souls into the jaws of hell.

NN5 The devil thrusting the condemned into the bottomless pit.

NN6 The devil leading the condemned captive.

NN7 The drunkards everlasting doom.

NN8 A figure rises from a coffin and three others rise from the dead around the coffin

NN9 An Angel conducting the righteous to glory.

NN10 The Last Judgement.

NN11 Trumpet Angel summoning mankind to the judgement.

NN12 Trumpet Angel summoning mankind to the judgement.

NN13 The resurrection unto life.

NN14 The resurrection unto damnation.

NN15 St Peter with the keys.

NN16 The resurrection of the just.

NN17 The resurrection of righteous women.

NN18 Three figures representing the persons of the Holy Trinity.

Bay NN2 New Testament
Bishop Walter Lyhart

The final three bosses adorn the top of the west window. Here Bishop Walter Lyhart the commissioning prelate is seen at prayer with censing angels either side of him. Bishop Lyhart replaced the previous wooden roof with a stone one containing all these wonderful bosses design by Reginald Ely. Lyhart's mason was Robert Everard who was in charge of works at the Cathedral from 1451 to 1485.

NN19 The effigy of Bishop Walter Lyhart who built the roof.

NN20 Angels adoring the Holy Trinity.

NN21 Angels adoring the Holy Trinity.

Acknowledgements

Firstly I would like to thank the Dean and Chapter of Norwich
Cathedral for allowing me to publish the photographs, also the staff at the
cathedral.
My thanks to Canon Phillip McFadyen for the use of his text on the
descriptions of the bays and their stories.
My thanks also to Barbara Hacker for editorial help with the text.

Bibliography

These books and articles will assist for studying the bosses.

The Very Rev'd Edward Merrick Goulburn, *Ancient sculptures in the roof of Norwich
Cathedral*

C J P Cave, *Roof Bosses in medieval Churhes,* Cambridge University Press.

Phillip McFadyen, *An Eye on Heaven,* Norwich Cathedral publications
ISBN 0 9535493-1-3

Martial Rose and Julia Hedgecoe, *Stories in Stone,* Thames and Hudson.
ISBN 0-500-27937-3

Website links

Paul Hurst ARPS - *www.dochurst.co.uk*

Norwich Cathedral - *www.cathedral.org.uk*

About Paul Hurst

PAUL HURST has over the last twenty years specialised in photography of Church and Cathedral architecture. Having been inspired by many years singing in the back benches of cathedral choirs he considers the strength of his work creates a visual link between the medieval media of the past and the digital one of today.

He illustrates books and exhibits his work in order to share his enthusiasm in the study of ancient art forms at greater depths. Paul is an Associate of the Royal Photographic Society and has had published articles in their Journal. Paul has recently engaged himself in publishing under the name of 'Medieval Media'.

By sharing his images more widely he hopes to stimulate greater interest in our medieval churches and encourage visitors to help maintain them for the enjoyment of future generations.